Accommodations

Accommodations

SARAH CAREY

Concrete Wolf
Chapbook Award Series

Copyright © 2019 Sarah Carey

All rights reserved. No part of this publication may be reproduced, distributed, or transmitted in any form or by any means whatsoever without written permission from the publisher, except in the case of brief excerpts for critical reviews and articles. All inquiries should be addressed to Concrete Wolf Press.

Concrete Wolf Chapbook Award Series

Poetry
ISBN 978-0-9964754-9-5

Design: Tonya Namura
using Gentium Basic and Colaborate

Cover photo by Sarah Carey

Author photo by Adrienne Fletcher

Concrete Wolf
PO Box 445
Tillamook, OR 97141

http://ConcreteWolf.com

ConcreteWolfPress@gmail.com

*I dedicate this book
in loving memory of my father,
John Jesse Carey,
for whom I will never have enough words for loss,
or gratitude.*

Table of Contents

An Ordinary Life	3
Letters Home	5
Heel of a Loaf	7
Seasonal Affective	9
Personal Cure for Consumption	11
Handkerchief	13
We Gather in Florida to Celebrate My Father's Life	14
The Changed Landscape	15
Personal Effects	16
Exploring Roots in the Hair Salon	18
First Day of Hurricane Season	19
Before Landfall	21
The Block House at Mexico Beach	23
Royal Palms Defend Their Place in the Condo Universe	25
Exotic Taste	26
Questions for the Plumber During Remodeling	28
Visualization	30
Ledger	31
Our Last House	32
Estate Planning	34
What I Tell My Unborn Children When They Ask Me Where I Come From	36
What We Carry	38
Paris Voices	40
At Rhine Falls	42
Acknowledgements	45
About the Author	47

Accommodations

An Ordinary Life

Not uprooted, not hunger-drawn,
never transplanted from my homeland,

I thrive within my native confines,

as a longleaf pine's armored bore
protects from fire and stores blood sap,

whose taproot mass drops anchor
beneath a grassy overstory—

told by my family so many times,

I've memorized even the smells
trade winds carried of their migration,
from their shore to mine—

fruitcake, from my German side,
roast beef and potatoes from my Irish—

when war or storm displaces
what we've earned in native soil,

we must revive our appetite for risk,

as memory fades, and we bank on spring,
while time, a careful surgeon,

debrides dead tissue from bole wounds,
forming a callus, allowing new growth

but hoped-for seedlings don't arrive.
Some of us migrate to survive,

but my inner flow feeds me,

channels my ancestors' endurance—
as I plant my feet, draw breath from toes
to gut, lungs to throat, all the way up,

claiming my brief space on earth,
like any native of this world.

Letters Home

In Russia, he hopped church to church,
couldn't get over the domes.

My father pens how bulbs were built
to shed snow, parsing every detail

at St. Basil's—its soaring, tented roof,
its fine iconostasis. Nine small chapels

aligned to compass points,
he internalized each nave

to recreate his journey for me,
scenes only he could script.

I picture, too, my sister ready to be born,
my father in a waiting room,

or by my mother's bed, beside himself,
head full of history, the next story

paused for the perfect delivery,
to show me the world again.

The past comes back as letters,
sky-blue, lighter than air, filed away

for decades, his familiar cursive
flown across the page, to alit the tale.

Until I knew my mother's labor
made his architecture true,

I couldn't see the view
he handed down,

mine to mine for clues
to our eventual unfolding.

Heel of a Loaf

My grandmother favored the heel,
shared Mother, when I asked
what she remembered of early meals,

as she passed peeled navel oranges,
soft-scrambled eggs at breakfast.
Now gluten-free, her twice-proven

loaves are history,
gone as our ancestors
yet stuck to our ribs forever.

Hunger must be relative, since we fasted
in my father's absence, each homecoming
a feast, as we lived our fantasies,

hot fudge sundaes—*Don't fill up on bread*,
he said, but left chocolate kisses
under pillows, cushioning his goodbyes.

These days, we stay preoccupied
with our long valediction: a growing cyst,
a deafened ear, or fading eye

we must have seen.
We circle doctor appointments,
sinking by degrees: one loses an insight,

another, a love. Mother's skin
grows thin, Sister's thickens—
but we rise to each occasion.

Home again, Alpha and Omega,
first and last of the children,
we claim our space at the table,

squeeze hands, as was our tradition,
give thanks, and *Amen.*

Seasonal Affective

My father's voice booms in on the second ring,
as if he never stopped speaking,

as if his words had never wavered,
or slurred. *He's fine,* we say, returning

to dismantling wreaths, stowing
away another holiday season's bling,

habituated to the shorter, darker days,
but keeping reasons to hope on display.

When he falls again, before winter ends,
and EMTs reset him in his wheelchair,

weren't we past this, we ask? Always no,
we say, and the chill extends to our bones

but when we hear seasons affect mood,
we pack our bags and fly, turning our backs

on cold, to meet spring on a beach,
where we let our healing hopes lap over us

like waves that touch us gently, then recede.
We dream we tell the children we can't have

to build a castle, as if the wet sand could teach
youth's grasping hands patience, or love

of form's impermanence. *There, there,*
we say, as if to keep loss at bay,

as if they lost only a season,
when their dreams wash away.

Personal Cure for Consumption

Fell out of a 4th floor window while sleepwalking
the death certificate said, though suicide
and post-traumatic stress were never speculated.

Only war, disease, act of God or accident
were ever discussed. *Tragedy struck that family,*
my mother said. Marshall's hardscrabble,

scribbled hardships, personal cure for consumption,
noted in letters Daisy left, brought home the war,
to all of us, who look for whys in ancestors,

whose ways we might inherit. Great-grandmother
Daisy kept her one son Marshall's memory green,
in papers I later parsed for clues, paging

through his darkness. I, too, drank. Nearly jumped,
a time or two. We might have shared
a fear of aging, or the same bleak dream.

Often I read too much into things—
but how can I not see the gray,
pretend to not know how he died?

A tragedy, my mother said, and said again,
when Marshall's niece, a newlywed, bled out,
kicked in the gut by a horse—

yet she has medicine in her voice, apothecary tales.
Daisy outlived losses till they swallowed her,
and she became them. She prescribes a bitter pill.

*Take this history morning, bedtime, or as needed,
with a grain of salt. You are more than DNA,*
she assuages, shakes me free.

Handkerchief

The linen square grazes a drawer lip,
settles like a sigh in the dark.

When I rise again and dress,
assess possibilities with my opening breath,
all the cherry chest holds realigns,

the burgundy monogram relaxes
as a grieving head nestles a beloved shoulder.

I palm it—pang of past tense, void of color,
as my father's face, pale at the end—
I cover mine, breathe him in.

If creases are laugh lines,
blotters of tears, if I carry as tightly,

as lightly the years, this wedding keepsake,
wrinkled remembrance, I can conjure

a tale, unfold a history,
comforting as Irish tradition, passed
from my grandmother, to Father, to me.

We Gather in Florida to Celebrate My Father's Life

Outside our hallway, cross-hatched
feathers, a flutter away from the hotel window,
perched hunter of the forest understory,

a red-shouldered hawk's eyes
meet our own, a window into which

we can't quite see, yet make our way—
third floor to first—open to story
after story, while outside a single magnolia,

gold-leafed in sun, backlights the first bloom,
as spring rain greens the asphalt oasis.

We greet our blood, catch up, cousins
lament cousins outlived, out of touch,
who moved, who stayed, despite the odors

of smoke or strangers—reconstruct
commitments made, unmade, pursued,

as time realigned our views.
I give up my ghosts, and everything I know
of human nature, which is nothing.

My father is salt and mineral, crushed bone.
We arrange to arrange to arrange.

Did you know, I told the gathered group,
flowers from each state he lived in flank the pulpit,
bloom today in all of them, in all of you:
dogwood, peony, forget-me-not.

The Changed Landscape

After office colleagues leave,
having talked over your head,

I dust your frame, arm's length away,
notice the magnolia tree behind you

blossoming despite the chill,
your eyes smiling beneath a felt fedora,

facing me focusing my lens,
never knowing I'd find you again

in my room each day,
across our weathered years—

frozen in that moment,
or that I'd scan, digitize,

then encase your print in glass
to protect you from the elements.

When I learn the magnolia's
Chinese ancestors programmed it

to bloom in the cold, the scene
unfolds with a fresh perspective:

snow by blossom, sunshine, stomata,
Asia by way of Decatur, now by then,

breathing in the past
to breathe again.

Personal Effects

We shattered the frozen lock,
in minus-ten degrees,

to inventory the life my father left,
when, finally well enough to travel,

with all he could fit in a suitcase,
he fled Alaska for the lower forty-eight.

We were there, but not all there.
Some of us were missing

a list to lean on—but listless at the end,
he assumed we would devise intent

in his stored things—
or in *shivelight lances,* Hopkins might say,

beamed at table leaves and lithographs,
a file case full of sermons.

I am unprepared for what I covet:
a stack of hats, a set of stationery,

the passport expired last year,
absent a single stamp.

Hope springs eternal, he quoted.
I'll take it all, on faith.

He might have considered Germany
again, or Ireland for the third time,

or left us a simple will to keep going.
A sister spots a carved pill box,

opens the hidden, dovetailed lid
on the nothing she'll fly home,

to house her own remembrances,
a fresh inheritance for no child to find.

Exploring Roots in the Hair Salon

My father's dead one year today,
but I am keeping my appointments,

recapping the reasons
I can't go to grey or ash just yet—
caped, colored and cut, I remember

when my stylist told me
there'd be a time to grow out my roots,

allowing thick to thrive, to throb untamed,
or at least uncultivated,
giving a name to this phase:

wild hair, as if it might be better then
than now, to abandon social mores,

as if I'd comb through grief
more easily, controlled,
avoiding unwanted attention.

Low lights, I tell her, *let's go with the bob*
that worked for both of us most years—
it feels like home to me.

My father teased
my sisters and I made him gray,
but he lost all his hair in the end.

I say keep me in the club of the well-coiffed,
slightly sprayed, with all that body
someone could bury their face in.

First Day of Hurricane Season

The bay's so low, the viewfinder
focuses ripple, flow above sand,

where your eye holds steady.
You count shells, wish for a zoom

to expand the panorama, revealing
a manatee's scarred hide, a graphite blur

in shallows. Some observe
survival drops in extreme storms,

a barometer of being, calm omen,
but we see preparation of a threatened species.

Tight flocks of gulls circle,
seek shelter in algae-covered rocks,

and wait, as sea currents intensify,
spin squalls into the bay's mouth.

Breaking news reports midnight landfall,
but at sunset, enthralled, we linger.

Ocean sediments will stay roiled
for weeks before they settle,

but I hit bottom,
and learned acceptance, long ago.

Breathe the slow wind—
another storm is always coming.

Imagine the world the great eye
will pass over, the world

hurricane and human nature
will leave behind.

Before Landfall

In the latest projection, Irma fingers
the spine of Florida's supine peninsula.

We track her path northwest on weather apps
from our safe room, where we lie on sleeping bags,

imagine protection looks like this: doors, windows
shut tight, radio, flashlight, disaster plans at hand.

Minutes away, the winds pick up.
The first rainbands deluge our roof.

Once again, we wait for havoc:
crashing trees, transformer arcs,

for the house to tremble
as freight train sounds roar through,

as if to make up for lost time,
fast-forwarding to an unknown end.

As the fluids left my father's body,
I watched him track my tears, a salt river,

smelling of seaweed and grief.
His good eye would see me through

just one more storm, the mopping up I'd do,
so sure we'd not be swamped again.

When I was as tiny as a country
seen from light years away, he held me

high above the swirling sea, that was
the beginning and the end of everything.

The Block House at Mexico Beach

He might have hunkered down, we said,
after all, he conquered tetanus as a child—

a story we hear long after the nail-hole
in his foot healed, after lockjaw's slow reveal.

Our stepfather blew through Chattahoochee,
squalled, made landfall at Mexico Beach,

a quiet town few knew back then,
settled into a cinderblock house,

on a pine-lined street my sister called an escape route
from the county no one ever left,

but children of his own still lived,
where nothing was forgiven or built back.

Call him our family evacuee. We let him be.
Still standing! I say to my husband, after the hurricane

swept through, zooming the aerial map
for the shine of his roofline's weathered steel,

amidst a city's leveled silhouette. We made peace
with what he couldn't tell us

years before he died, before the worst storm came,
before old neighbors battened hatches, prayed,

but we relived his stay-or-leave dilemmas
and their hold on us, when we found the house

shuttering his everlasting secrets.

Memories flood our consciousness—

familiar blasts of cooler air in fall, his long-dead cats,
our oceanfront hotel, a ritual, now blown away

as signs of normalcy we grieve anew,
once we view them flattened.

Royal Palms Defend Their Place in the Condo Universe

We have heard our pinnate fingers terrify
your board, whose members mouth our roots reach deep
enough to threaten your foundation.

Others can address our penetration,
but our landscape virtues are renowned,
our crowns ubiquitous, in climates just this warm,

and warmer, south. We impede some views, it's true,
but the association knew, or should have known,
our nature when we went to ground—

every snowbird's paradise incarnate,
yet how could we have known, we'd grow
beyond your expectations,

to thrum our fan blades against your panes, letting you see
us as we are: inhuman royals,
who must reach for creature comfort, still,

to justify our space, must seek the beating next to us
that makes us one, beside our own bud heart,
from which all new leaves come.

Exotic Taste

Where was I when the fabricator told us
he could scan remodeling plans,

colorize, digitize them to bring home
the best cuts from our granite slabs?

After reviewing the countertop layout,
you objected to the lack of river

in our vanity, how someone put
uniformity over flow.

After all, we chose Typhoon Bordeaux
for movement, rich energy. Tell me,

dear husband, how we became engaged
so passionately about a stone.

Drawing over drawings, you convey
your views, bathroom to cooktop,

where to cut, to save
regret, hone compromise.

I struggle to grasp. Look away.
It's not that I don't listen, I do.

Now, you try: slabs quarried in Brazil
we thought became us—queue

a sawyer, a savior for exotic taste,
carving space for books and elbows,

shelves for vases, toiletries,
cards of sympathy and thanks.

Our house evokes a world,
perfect as Marvell's drop of dew,

and as congealed, our heaven-less on Earth,
reflected in our island's sealed, polished face.

Questions for the Plumber During Remodeling

If I guess correctly that we need
to clear out the old,

to make room for the new,

can you please tap the pipes,
tone-test for sounds of blockage?

Could you un-clog our processes—

teeth-brushing, counter wipes,
elimination of each day's waste,

how we cook, clean and dress,

that we might come and go
more fluidly?

Would you please take a snake

to remove whatever drags
our course-by-rote mid-torrent?

We flowed through other homes

we threw everything into,
including the kitchen sink,

which might have sunk us—

tore down walls in each abode,
then second-guessed our openness.

We built an island, explored a radiant floor

to warm us from the ground up,
floated enclosed concepts.

Before you clean the traps, please augur

through whatever obstructs us,
catheterize our plaque, or egos,

set it all free, so we may flow.

Visualization

Beneath where upper cabinets
corner backsplash, wires protrude,
like untamable curls, beside their not-yet outlets,

where old knives could rest anew: bird's beaks,
serrated breads, filets, one chef,
a cleaver, all my steaks.

Conjure the bubbling coffee brewing
beside the fridge, timer beeping you
into the next task, waiting as you have,

eager to be occupied, preoccupied,
with all who came and went inside a space,
who could have stayed, but didn't.

We're not there yet, says the builder,
eyeballing kerfs at toe kicks, holes in drywall,
managing our expectations, but already,

I'm lining shelves, cutting butter
into flour, beating milk, eggs, baking soda
into batter, racking pans. When I break in the oven

to convect, you'll forget the grief you spent,
not eating when your father died. All we paid

for what we craved, our second chance.
We'll start again in softer light, in which we'll see
each other, aging in the stainless.

Ledger

We review the budget, cell by cell:
overages in cabinets, tile and stone, bleed

into margins to track fault, reconcile
the zeros of embellishment,

and bare bones. *We were satisfied,*
we told the builder, clicking through

the punch list—happy not to move again,
noting every blemish smoothed to perfection,

each room's fresh illusion of space,
regenerating us, cell by cell, dollar by dollar.

Though we bought new dishes,
we preferred the old stoneware, selected

when we wed for life, an inventory
of inverse proportion, less to do

with net worth, than remembrance
of our origins, of choices that survive us.

You say we've never
lived beyond our means,

by which you mean
we're justified.

Our Last House

From country to city, student ghetto
to suburban enclave, plotting
where we fit, we finally land

west of town, home at last,
among slash pines and water oaks,
Chuck-will's-widow, baritoned owls.

After we change the paint
and rearrange the art, I claim,
This is the landscape we were meant to own.

We admired our water feature,
windmill palms inside the lanai.
How did it all grow old?

Perhaps we tired of being crepuscular,
having given up on loving all night long,
expecting day jobs to define us.

Or feared native grasses' failure
to thrive beneath trees, mildew
blackening our doors,

despite cleaning after cleaning,
diluting gallons of bleach
sweating bullets in the heat.

Perhaps the crack in the floor
that betrayed settling did us in. Did we
settle for too little in eschewing guests,

just us, and the house
we could set fire to, claiming accident,
or sell as is, but who would buy it?

We keep dusting and scrubbing,
now and then look up, admire our views,
weigh how much to disclose.

Estate Planning

When you asked me where we were,
with our wills and my advance directive,

I told you someone will always crave
the lost embrace, the felt thing,

impossible to give away or hold.
Always some aspect of belonging

eludes capture: the blood pressure cuff
still beeping its battery warning,

the rare laugh, with its octave of wheezes.
I could have said our joint accounts

were loans, illusory security, hunger a gift,
that clings to its beneficiaries. Instead,

I wished you'd take on my longing,
like a chore left incomplete when a shift

ends and a worker finally clocks out.
I gave all my want to you, and you returned it

with interest, a credit to society, a lot
in life. I'll leave you my best guess

of usefulness, the protocols and processes
that made my job my life, my life,

my love, my Darling. No words
can cover everything I couldn't tell you,

though you can't know yet what you
are missing. Where are we, you ask?

I write on the waiting paper, *Surrogate*,
your name, then—*breathe for me.*

What I Tell My Unborn Children When They Ask Me Where I Come From

Wherever I was, I spoke in the wrong tone and tongue, drew the wrong ears to my story, retold so you'd believe my words were mine alone, not endless strands of DNA bespeaking other passages: a train's maiden voyage to a promised land, the new bride wed to the young rail hand, who fell onto the track, crushed while cars were coupling.

This is not my language, but I hope you understand. In time, I saw my true conveyance: migrations swept me here from Ireland, England, Germany, onto farms I worked until the Western Carolina soil wore out, then into mines and textile mills, the lumber industry.

Hardy stock I got, but I could never settle, moved from relative to relative, to matter in your most nostalgic recollection, intuition's spark: mass of muscle memory, fantasy mother. I'd speak of manifested fullness, not barren but content, when I asked about regret. Some say what they'd do differently, if they could go back in time, but let me set the record straight:

Part of me broke in Roanoke, where great-uncle Marshall fell from a hotel window—*suicide*, my mother said, but the death certificate read *accident*. In my dreams, I shake the hand of the man who married Marshall's widow, gave her grandson a namesake. This was fate, I tell you. This was tenderness I can't swear you'll inherit.

Then I'd travel west to Indiana, where I'd ask my great-grandfather why his first wife left him, if he ever dreamed of getting even—or of me, the one he never knew, unearthing family secrets, articulating a tree. I share this, not to make magnificent my own small sacrifices, but to tell you true—I moved too fast, then, to marry.

What We Carry

Some things we took for granted vanished
long ago: a store, a mall, a whole shopping plaza,

an entire country we grew up in, moving
state to state, when welcome signs

marked the borders, and no one spoke
of red and blue intent, or waves to change

the nation's constitution. Remember when
we were blank slates, and midterms, examinations?

How did we outgrow our openness,
our eagerness to face the challenges we met?

If I give to you my oyster and my watch,
will you please be my witness?

We've survived shrinking human concern
for endangered species, carcinogens

in pesticides, too much ultraviolet,
refuse to say we live in a threatened habitat—

existing instead in separate fantasies
of what our lives used to be,

just as I'd be lying if I said I don't dream
our mail carrier will deliver to my cul-de-sac,

my father's aerograms, featherlight and blue
as air, his world flown back to me

across decades, and less polluted seas.
I see their ghostly envelopes

nestled with cards of sympathy,
congratulations, and friends' confessions.

All vanished in the internet's virtual wake.
Mailboxes open and close,

like gates to an abandoned land—
or bird mouths we hope to feed,

like airborne mothers,
sustenance to fly another day,

carrying what matters
to the next generation.

Paris Voices

Here, a ghostly murmur. There, a keen.
An undercurrent crosses continents
as we rise, morning-weak, sleep-deprived,

from bed, discuss our day,
what plans we've made for lunch,
if we'll venture to an evening play,

yet, wondering if our words will turn to prayer,
if a terrorist or Good Samaritan
comes to drag us from our avenue,

through office doors, lock us in
as hostages, or for protection,
if our fate will seal a country's cause,

or conjure an isolated incident—
imagine bloody concert halls,
juxtaposed against our former exuberance.

Later, outside a café,
a couple that dove to dodge bullets,
returns to a sea of tea lights, knee-deep

in strewn bouquets. A block away,
a rose decays in a broken window.
To seem to bloom, to not unravel,

I garland my neck in the gauzy scarf
I bought near the Louvre long ago,
when shopping overrode museums,

until the city drew its nightly veil.
How we laughed at how
we'd come home artless,

to a different darkness.
Now we turn, are turned upon,
consider a bus, ubiquitous,

the two of us, a world apart,
but not from anarchy,
or any human frailty.

At Rhine Falls

We wake to rain in our son's new country.
Layered in shell, windbreaker, fleece,

set out for Schloss Laufen: flower boxes,
food trucks vending Indian cuisine,

a courtyard packed for a castle wedding,
guests dressed in black and gray.

Bleuler taught painters here, inspired
a roomful of hanging landscapes,

as if to train our eyes to possibility, before we see.
We strain to read more history under glass,

then spiral down steep wet stone steps,
misty-faced, until the falls' roar stops us

hearing anything, but what artists,
barons, a bishop, and the last count

came for: hundreds of thousands of liters
of water, of years converged. An origin

story, tectonic shifts, cracked bedrock,
a flow of water an earthquake changed.

My pilgrim heart possessed, my face awash
with spray, I close my eyes, draw breath,

and press my step-grandson's hand,
which holds his father's firm,

as the pounding water scatters foam
  below us, lacy as the veil he may raise.

Acknowledgements

My sincere thanks to the editors of the journals that first published or acknowledged the following poems. The poems, sometimes in earlier versions, appeared as follows:

Alaska Women Speak: "We Gather in Florida to Celebrate My Father's Life" and "At Rhine Falls"; *Barrow Street:* "Our Last House"; *The Christian Century:* "Changed Landscape"; *Eyewear Publishing Fortnight Poetry Prize:* "We Gather in Florida to Celebrate My Father's Life", then titled "Accommodations," was a shortlisted finalist; *Glass Poetry Journal:* "Exploring Roots in the Hair Salon" and "What I Tell My Children When They Ask Me Where I Come From"; *Gravel:* "Royal Palms Defend Their Place in the Condo Universe"; *Palette Poetry:* "What We Carry"; *Potomac Review:* "Personal Effects"; *Rock Salt Plum Review:* "Letters Home"; *Sequestrum:* "An Ordinary Life" was a finalist in the 2018 New Writer Awards competition; *South Florida Poetry Journal*: "Personal Cure for Consumption"; *Superstition Review:* "Exotic Taste"; *SWWIM Every Day:* "Before Landfall"; *Tampa Tribune:* "First Day of Hurricane Season"; *UCityReview:* "Questions for the Plumber During Remodeling"; *Valparaiso Review:* "Paris Voices".

"Personal Cure for Consumption" is in memory of my great-uncle, Marshall Parsons. The Block House at Mexico Beach" is in memory of my stepfather, John D. Malloy.

I gratefully acknowledge Lola Haskins and April Ossmann for their expertise and help in honing the poems that make up this manuscript. Special thanks to kindred spirits Adam Houle and Hannah VanderHart for their generosity in sharing work and feedback. All my love and appreciation to my husband, Chad, for his ongoing understanding and support. To my mom, Sally Stanback Malloy, my sisters, and all the members of my extended family: I can't tell you what it means to have you in my corner every moment of every day.

About the Author

Sarah Carey is a North Carolina native, but grew up in Tallahassee, Florida. She attended Duke University and Florida State University, and received a Master of Arts degree in English with a concentration in creative writing/poetry from FSU in 1981.

One of the poems from her creative thesis was a finalist in the Academy of American Poets competition, and in the final year of her graduate program, Sarah had her first poetry publication in the *Florida Review*.

Her poems have appeared in *Carolina Quarterly, Rattle, Valparaiso Review, Potomac Review, Glass Poetry Journal, SWWIM Every Day, Rise Up Review, Palette Poetry* and many others. She received an International Merit Award in the 2018 *Atlanta Review* International Poetry Competition, and was a finalist in *Sequestrum Literary Journal*'s 2018 New Writer Award competition.

Sarah spent ten days as a residency-only student at the MFA program for writers at Warren Wilson College in Swannanoa, N.C. in 1987 and later participated in two Key West Writer's Workshops with the poet Carolyn Forché.

In addition to this collection, she is the author of the poetry chapbook, *The Heart Contracts,* published in 2016 by Finishing Line Press.

While in college, Sarah waited tables, wrote copy for the local public television station and covered news and features for the student newspaper. After completing her graduate studies, Sarah began working for weekly newspapers in the Florida Panhandle, becoming one of the state's youngest-ever newspaper editors when she was named editor of the *Gadsden County Times* in 1983 at the age of 25. Many of her stories were honored with awards from organizations including the Florida Press Association, the Florida Press Club, and the Florida Medical Association.

In 1990, she began working for the University of Florida College of Veterinary Medicine, where she remains today as director of communications, routinely writing and publicizing stories on topics ranging from clinical advances benefiting pets, exotic animals, horses and livestock, to biomedical discoveries affecting animal, human and environmental health. Sarah's public relations work has received several awards from the Florida Public Relations Association, which named her its Jack M. Detweiler Professional of the Year in 2012.

Sarah lives in Gainesville, Florida. Visit her at sarahkcarey.com, or on Twitter @SayCarey1.

www.ingramcontent.com/pod-product-compliance
Lightning Source LLC
Chambersburg PA
CBHW030458010526
44118CB00011B/997